HOW DO FOSSILS FORM?

THE EARTH'S HISTORY IN ROCKS

Children's Earth Sciences Books

BABY PROFESSOR
EDUCATION KIDS

Speedy Publishing LLC
40 E. Main St. #1156
Newark, DE 19711
www.speedypublishing.com

Long before there were people, it was the age of the dinosaurs. They ruled the earth for over 150 million years. But they are long gone, and we mostly learn about them now through the fossil record. What's a fossil? Read on and find out!

Fossil at Tham Pha Tha Pon Wildlife Sanctuary, Noen Maprang Phitsanulok, Thailand.

WHAT'S A FOSSIL?

When animals, plants, insects and other organisms die, their remains usually disappear over time. They break down into the minerals and other elements that they were made of and those elements return to the Earth and eventually get reused for other plants and animals, or for rocks or even other odd things!

But if the conditions are just right, the animal, plant, or insect doesn't go away completely. Parts or even most of it get preserved for us to admire millions of years later. Usually they get preserved as fossils.

Imprint of an ancient mollusk on a rock. Crimea.

HOW DO FOSSILS HAPPEN?

Animals and plants can become fossils in several different ways. Each way is very slow, and depends on the conditions being just right. Most of the time, animal and plant remains just break down and get recycled by the Earth without leaving a trace.

FREEZING, DRYING AND ENCASEMENT

Around 1900, people in northern Siberia found a whole mastodon, an elephant-like creature, frozen in the ice. It was preserved so well that scientists could explore the contents of its stomach and figure out what it was doing just before it died. Not only that, the mastodon was in such a good shape of preservation that some of its meat was cut up, prepared, and served at a special dinner hosted by the Czar of Russia!

Most of the time, remains from ancient days are not so recognizable, or tasty. However, not all of the creatures and plants from the age of the dinosaurs either died by freezing or were frozen into ice not long after their deaths. For some, their bodies gradually desiccated, or dried out, but their bones, the structure of their internal organs, and often their skin, fur or feathers were preserved.

Brachiopod Fossils closeup.

Near Los Angeles in the United States there is a famous site called the La Brea Tar Pits. Even millions of years ago this was an open area of tar and oil. Many dinosaurs wandered into tar pits like this around the world, were unable to escape, and were gradually encased by the tar. The tar hardened around them and preserved their bones, though not normally their soft tissues.

Fossil shell in marble.

Amber is a semi-precious jewel made out of fossilized resin, or sap, from ancient trees. Sometimes in a piece of amber is a wing or leg of an ancient insect that got stuck in the resin and had to leave a body part behind. Very rarely, there is a whole prehistoric mosquito or other insect!

Resin, gum.

Fossil plants in carbonaceous shale

CARBONIZATION

Sometimes the combination of heat and pressure working on the remains of a plant or an animal buried in sediment—at the bottom of a stream, for instance—can be just right for a process called "carbonization" or "distillation". The tissues of the organism break down and dissolve, but as they do they release hydrogen and oxygen...and leave behind a little remainder of carbon.

The carbon that remains leaves a detailed image of the dead organism. As the sedimentary material hardens into rock, over a very long time, the detailed image is trapped in the rock like a snapshot of a creature from our past.

When scientists find these carbonization images, they don't have the original organism to work with. But they have an image of the creature or plant. They can learn whether it had fur or feathers—or maybe both! What were its wings like? If it was a plant, did it have thorns and what was the shape of its leaves?

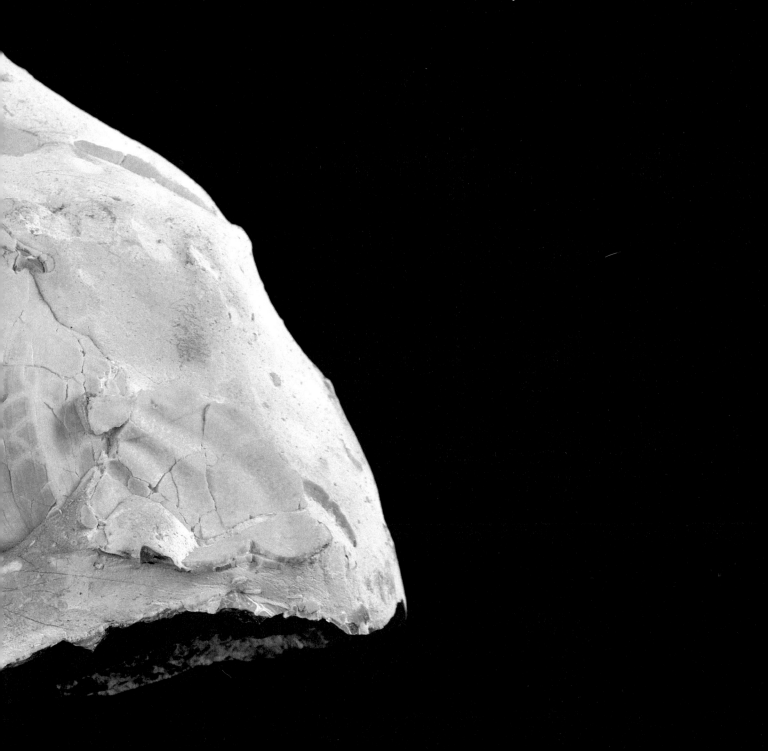

Petrified shell Inoceramus in flint. Palecepoda. Kremenets, Ukraine.

PETRIFICATION

By far the most frequent way that fossils are created is through petrification—the remains of the organism turn into a rock, or into a rocky image of the thing that is no longer there.

Petrification has several steps and takes a very, very long time. Let's go over the steps that might lead from a living dinosaur to a fossil in a museum.

Winged Ant Dominican Amber Fossil

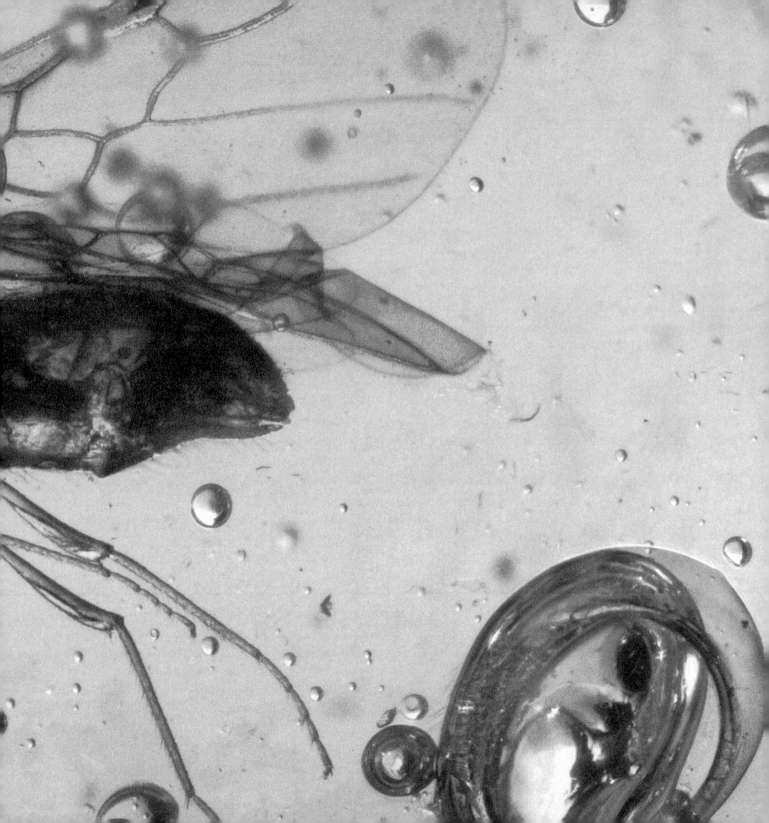

THE ANIMAL DIES

When most animals die, their body parts are consumed by other animals. But sometimes an animal dies in or near the sea, a lake, or a river. Its body sinks to the bottom of the water.

Fish, insects and small animals eat some of the soft parts of the animal, bacteria and other tiny creatures eat more, and the rest rots away. Only the skeleton is left. Slowly the sediment buries the skeleton.

Over time, the crust of the earth shifts and changes, sometimes due to plate tectonics, volcanic action, earthquakes, pressure from glaciers, and other events. If the skeleton is on the bottom of a lake or the sea, it sinks down as the earth's surface below the water sinks down. Pressure increases on the sediment, and over time it turns hard. It becomes sedimentary rock. Read the Baby Professor book *Metamorphic, Igneous, and Sedimentary Rocks: Sorting Them Out* to learn more about sedimentary rocks.

information

THE BONES DISSOLVE

Through cracks in the rock, water finds its way to the skeleton and slowly, slowly dissolves the bones. This leaves a space where the bones were, in the shape of the bones. Very little of the bone material remains.

Fossils on the beach of Dorset England.

MINERALS ARRIVE

As water rich in minerals follows the original ground water, it washes through the hollow spaces and deposits some of its minerals. Slowly a cast, or copy, of the original skeleton builds up. It is a copy, in rock and other minerals, of the long-gone bones.

The internal organs and the skin of the creature are long gone, so most of the time we have no idea of what was on the inside or the outside of the animal's bones!

Exposed fossil of a trilobite on a fossilized sediment plate.

A fossil of an unidentified fish in Jordan.

A FOSSIL EMERGES

Millions of years pass. Plate tectonics, earthquakes, the rising of mountains and the changing of seas and rivers continue their work of reshaping the surface of the Earth.

Because of these changes, a part of the Earth's surface that was once under water starts to rise up as part of a mountain or the edge of a continent. Our fossil is inside that new mountain or cliff.

Over a very long time wind, water, the actions of plants and the passage of other animals work on the sedimentary rock, slowly wearing it away. One day a little bit of the skeleton is exposed to the light of day. That's when someone walking by may notice it, investigate it, and realize they are looking at a marvellous thing from our distant past!

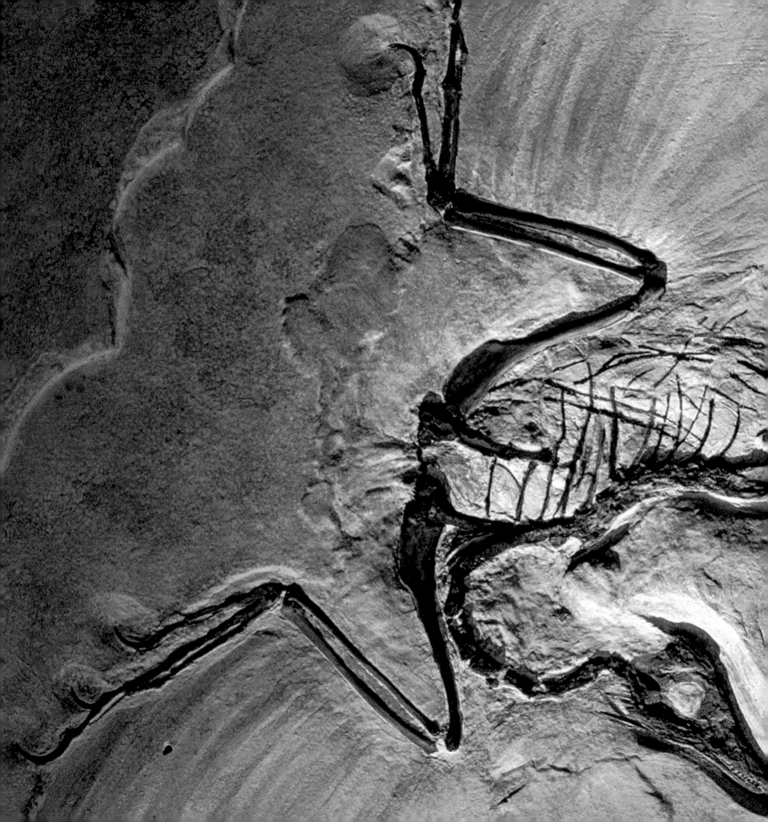

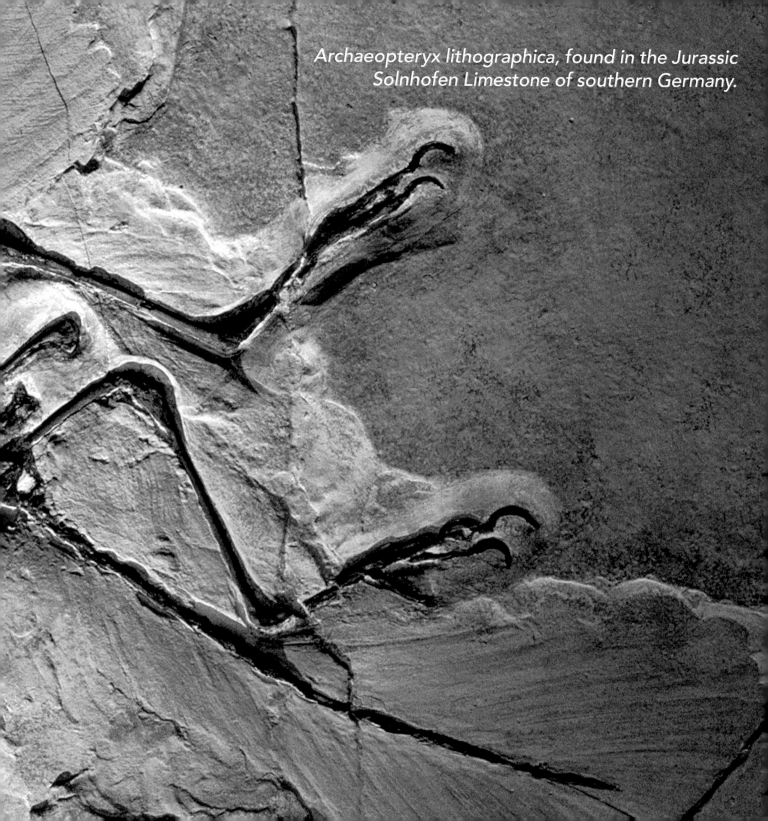
Archaeopteryx lithographica, found in the Jurassic Solnhofen Limestone of southern Germany.

WHAT FOSSILS TELL US

Fossils can show us a lot about gigantic creatures who lived long before humans existed. They can show us the shape, strength, and arrangement of the bones of a creature we have never seen before.

From those bones we can figure out many things. Was this a creature with a long neck? If so, why did he need such a long neck? Was he eating off the tops of trees like a giraffe?

And then we dig a bit further where we found the first bones and we find bones that indicate that this creature didn't have feet, but flippers! Now we know it was a swimming dinosaur, and maybe used its long neck to eat things off the bottom of the sea it lived in.

ORGANIC REMAINS?

Almost all the time, the fossils we find are made up of minerals that have replaced what made up the animal's bones. But recently scientists have found that sometimes some organic material lingers. Scientists have shown that the proteins in this material matches some of the proteins in modern birds. Modern birds evolved from dinosaurs.

An early sea creatures fossil.

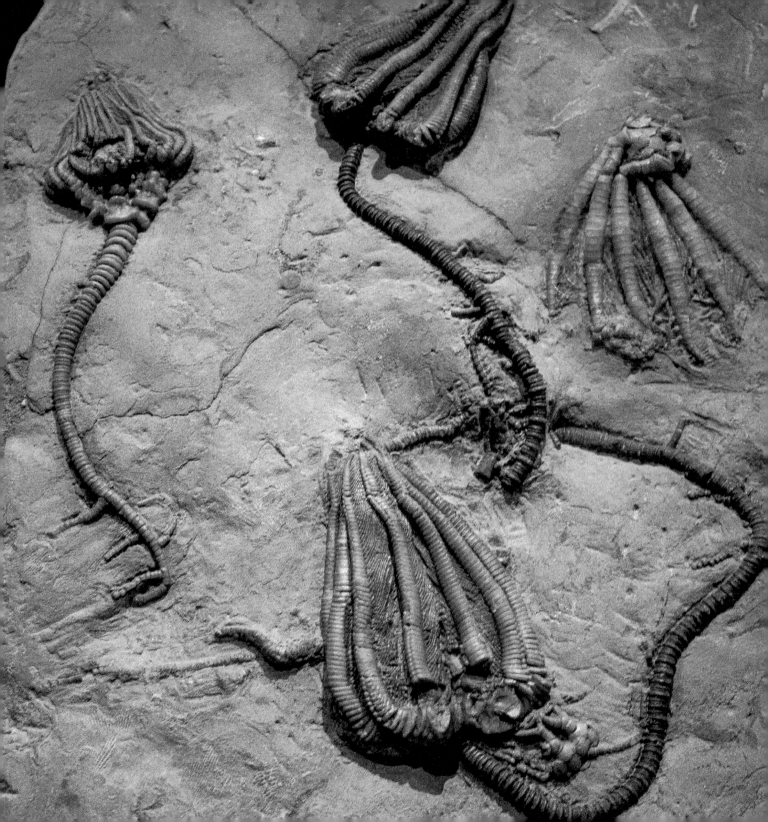

Ammonite Fossil Shell.

But to a microbe there are lots of highways and paths through the sandstone. So it's possible that microbes can get more quickly to a skeleton in sandstone, and consume it more quickly while there is still some organic material to leave behind.

Nobody is quite sure what preserves this organic material, but it might happen most easily when there is a lot of iron in the water that seeps into the space and dissolves the skeleton's bones. It's also possible that the bacteria that feed on the skeleton leave behind some of the bones' material as their own waste.

Minerals. Agate and ammonit.

Another possibility has to do with the nature of sandstone. Sandstone is made of bits of minerals and other materials the size of grains of sand you might see at the beach, all pressed together. To us, they seem very small and a piece of sandstone looks like pretty solid rock.

Marine biology.

THERE IS MUCH MORE TO LEARN

Dinosaurs were amazing, and ruled the Earth for over 150 million years! Read Baby Professor books like *The Big Dino-pedia for Small Learners* to learn more about dinosaurs.

Visit

BABY PROFESSOR
EDUCATION KIDS

www.BabyProfessorBooks.com

to download Free Baby Professor eBooks
and view our catalog of new and exciting
Children's Books